soft.

ISBN-13: 978-1-949191-01-1

Jeanius Publishing LLC
430 Lee Blvd
Lehigh Acres, FL 33936

For more information, please visit:
Jeaniuspublishing.com

soft.

Kiana Azizian

Jeanius
PUBLISHING

soft
/sôft/
(adjective)

not firm or hard to touch.

to be kind, beautiful, and humane.

one who is delicate, caring, and gentle.

soft is not weak.

to be soft is to be strong.
to be soft is to be unstoppable.

somehow,
i am
soft
yet
rigid,
all at
the
same
time.

- human

soft

the
hardening.

Kiana Azizian

this hardening was
not a part of the plan.
it came out of nowhere,
and knocked the wind
out from my lungs.
it left me breathless,
dazed,
lost.
confused.
then the darkness took over,
and it changed me;
ripping apart the soft creature i used to be.
they don't warn us about the pain,
or the grief that lives with it.
but even worse,
they do not teach us
how to deal with it all.
how to cope,
grieve the grief,
forgive the hurt.
soften the parts that we
have lost to the hardening.

i know what you've been through,
i've been around the same places.
i thought you looked familiar.
the pain,
it lives in your eyes.
trying to escape with each tear.
every drop telling a story of its own.
you fell in love,
didn't you?
tell me all about them.
you are safe here.
were they everything you'd hoped for,
perhaps even a little more?
did they say all the right things
at the right time?
were they pure perfection?
you'd do anything for them,
i know, i know.
like i said,
i've been there too.
but they left.
without any proper closure,
gone before the dusk of night.
your poor heart,
i can hear the cracks as it beats.
it has seen better days.
they took so much of you,
now you're not even sure who you are without
their existence in your life.
you're still mourning the loss of them,
the loss of yourself.
i know it must be hard to see the bigger picture
right now...

all you can imagine is
how flawlessly they walked away,
replaying all the promises said,
all the promises made.
but listen closely.
them leaving was the
best thing to ever happen to you.
thank them.
this is all you owe them.
be grateful for their departure,
because the day they left,
was also the day
you were reminded
how important it is to truly admire,
and put yourself first.
forever.
and always.

i just want you
and your wild love.

soft

love that stays.

this is the type
of love i crave.

- infinite

you taste like a dream.

*i never want to wake
up from you.*

*- **cloud nine***

your eyes tell me
all i need to know.
i can already
foreshadow
the way your touch
will ruin me.
please don't come
any closer.
stay away from me.
you reek of my
next mistake.

people
come and go.

but you.
you have
always stayed.

- permanent

*love like
you doesn't
come around
very often.*

- thankful

none of this,
life,
has made
any sense,
until you.

soft.

kissing your lips for
the first time felt
like the earth stopping.
it was mouth-parting,
heart-captivating,
jaw-dropping.
it was a
spectacular phenomenon.

- utopia

you taste
like the light
i've been
seeking.

i think you
are my sun.

- you are my day

his calmness has
overridden my chaos.
it's true what they
say about opposites,
they do attract.

soft.

i am lost in the art of loving you.

i was a ship.
he was the sea.

shipwreck was
inevitable.

- *collision*

*i slowly sunk
into you.
it was easier than
facing myself.*

- ***identity***

love me deeply.

i want to drown
into you.

i'd never consider
myself an addict,
well,
until you.
the night sweats
come without notice,
uncontrollable itching.
this skin barely
fits me anymore.
you have become
more than a desire.
a necessity.
essential for living.
i want you,
has become
an understatement.

i need you.

soft.

i want to learn the language of your spine.

get out before it's too late,
my mind is raging.

give it a chance,
my heart is begging.

you taste like childhood,
recognizable scents,
and lasting memories.
you feel like the
excitement of growing up,
learning the flow of life.
you feel like
coming home
after days,
months,
years,
away.
you are like unexplored
fields of sunflowers,
first kisses under the
light of the stars,
the lingering scent
of campfire smoke.

you are familiar,
yet like nothing
i've ever
experienced
before.

oh how he
puts the light
into the day.

i cannot
bring myself
to just
walk away.

i've marked you
a spot in my heart,
i'll treasure you with
each and every pulse.

- chest of treasure

*my love is
the ocean.*

*you must learn
to swim in the
waves of my soul,
or plunge
in all the chaos
which lives in
my heart.*

- sink or swim

you are the peace i crave in this chaotic world.

soft.

the first time
you laid
your hands
upon me,
i thought you
were made of
pure gold.

- *gem*

*every time i gained
a piece of you,
i lost a piece of me.*

- ***a willing sacrifice***

your eyes became
my vision,
your mouth became
my source of air.
your body became
my haven,
your soul became
my shelter.

when all was
said and done,
i didn't even know
who i was anymore.
you left me behind,
feeling disoriented
in my own body.
breathless.
gone,
tired and terrified.

and now,
i am lost at the
very thought of
your sacred name.

he made
me soft again.
kind and humble.
forgiving.
he has brought
me to my knees,
and reminded me
the beauty of
being grounded.

gradually i began
to fall for you,
hesitant every
step of the way.
it's been so long,
i've omitted what passion
is supposed to feel like.
your youthful touch
overtakes me,
compelling my soul.
you steal my bones,
unravel my spine
until i am
completely undone.
bare.
raw.
pure honey and flesh
lying on your
white, silk sheets.
you don't call me
beautiful.
you called me
heavenly;
a goddess.

before you,
i thought
love was chaotic.
madness.
fire and flames.
i thought love
was a battlefield.
war.
a death wish.
i thought love was
sleepless nights.
no appetite.
nonfunctional.
but loving you was
everything but torture.
loving you was easy.
simple.
graceful.
loving you was the
most natural thing
i have ever consumed.
loving you was
like breathing,

it was effortless.

you blow straight through me,
yet shake up my domain.
thunder cracks and
lightning strikes every time
i hear your name,
storms brew inside my soul
when you're near.
i haven't been myself
since you've appeared.

soft.

his lips are
a burning gun.

i love taking
bullets from him.

you've been through a lot,
i can see it in your eyes.
you've got a big heart,
and you're not sure
what to do with all of it.
you've given too much of yourself
to people who weren't worth it.
the people who promised
to never hurt you,
did,
and the ones who promised
to never leave,
left without even a
proper caution of their departure.
you know where you want to be in life,
yet can't find the road
which will lead you there.
you're lost,
truly misplaced.
unsure of your direction,
and not sure where to go next.
caught in-between being
afraid of repeating the past,
and wrecking the future.
you must understand,
it gets better.
your past doesn't define you,
and your future remains unmarked.
just because you've been hurt before,
doesn't mean you will hurt again.
people leave.
but sometimes people come back.
stop searching for what you are not,
and start loving everything
you have become.

for some reason,
his eyes don't sparkle
like the stars anymore.

- dull

*once it was over,
i kind of missed
his sad eyes
and wicked lies.*

- confession

you don't taste like you used to,
or touch me in the right places.
you don't kiss me with that
thirsty look in your eyes.
we have changed.
i'm not sure where to go from here.
we act like lovers,
yet are hardly in love anymore.
sticking to our scripts,
we play our parts without
having to practice our lines.
hitting each cue,
every scene is perfection.
eloquent.
the audience
is convinced of our roles.
i'm so tired of this performance.
it's time to throw in the towel,
and call it a show.

we made this place our home.
painted the walls red,
flowered them with photographs
of remarkable memories.
our lives spelled out with
the mess of worn clothes,
and cluttered belongings.
it all looks perfect from the outside,
but we tiptoe around each other lately,
guests in our own home.
ghosts too afraid of being seen,
noticed.
we stick to our own sides of the bed now,
not crossing borders without permission,
clearance.

every night,
you whisper
i love you,
and i can't help but think
this is out of habit,
not sincerity.

and all I ever needed was for you to fight for me.

soft.

i wouldn't
call what we
had love.

i would call
it madness.

- i would call it chaos

she's changed.
you can see it in her eyes,
feel it in her touch,
hear it in her tone.

she's not the same.
and she's never coming back.

*- **because you've lost her***

i guess i'm the only
one left with the blame.
you warned me of
your destructive manner,
but i was too stubborn
to get out of your way.

you're nothing but arbitrary
words on these crumbled pages.
a faint lingering memory,
one that never completely fades.
dissipates.
stagnant water under
a neglected bridge.
disremembered photographs in
a run-down shoebox.
a slight discomfort in the
cavity of my lungs.

one day,
i'll be able to walk out to
the ledge and not be afraid to swim,
and not fear the possibility of
suffocating your wake.

but for now,
i'll hold on to the little pieces
of yourself you left behind.
because this is the only
thing getting me through.

your lies were comforting.
they sounded like
a melody i've heard
hundreds of times before.
they tucked me into bed,
kissed my forehead,
rocked me throughout
the night.
they created my
favorite lullaby.
naively i wanted to
know your truth,
but it seems
some deceits are better
left misunderstood.

soft.

it's 3:37 a.m.,
silence is all
i hear from you.

it's so loud in here.

i need to get
some sleep.

you didn't even
realize i was there
until i was absent.
so detached.
distant.
overlooking the thing
standing in front of you,
you were too
focused on the past.
you didn't have
eyes for the future.

i cannot keep praying
you will come back home to me.
my hands are getting tired,
grasping on to this thread
you've kept me
reeled on.
i've never been so
afraid of heights,
standing out on this edge,
scared of what lies ahead.
you promised to catch me,
but you're nowhere to be found.

maybe it's time for me to let go,
and hope my wings have
grown strong enough to help me fly.

i will not blame you
for taking advantage
of all the chances
i handed you.
just as i will not blame
myself for being
so reckless with
my fragile heart.

let's call it even.

i have unintentionally
convinced myself
i am not worthy of
compassion.

- death sentence

*my biggest regret
in life is convincing
myself you would be
the end of me.*

- but you were not

i'm always hoping you might
come back around to me.
this house is no home
without your touch.
it's just four bare walls,
which have seen too much,
yet felt so little.

he was in love
with my idea,
not me.
i could see it
in his eyes.
they never
lied to me.
they always
told the truth,
unlike him.

i miss you,
but i'm not sure how to tell you.
so i'll sit with my thoughts,
and the stinging void
you have given me,
trying to compose
the words to help
articulate how nothing
feels the same without you.
sometimes i wish you'd come back,
but i cannot keep holding
on to something so far gone.

he only left a
few months ago,
but he's been
gone for years.

- absent

*i'm exhausted
from not being
seen by the
eyes i've fallen
in love with.*

- overlooked

i've packed up your things,
especially your memories,
and left them out
by the front door.
don't bother knocking,
i've changed the locks,
and hidden the spare key.
how does it feel standing
behind shut doors?
i've been doing so for months.
i've finally decided to move on.
let go.
and i think it's time
you do so as well.

soft.

maybe love and i weren't made for one another.

i've spent too much of my
precious time and energy on men
who didn't deserve my love.
draining this massive heart,
which fragilely sits
within the thin cage of my bruised ribs.
i apologize in advance
to the man who comes next,
because i'm not sure what i have to give.
all of my warmth has been scattered in the ones
who i was trying to create into him.

i hope i can find it within
myself to love him as he deserves.

i don't feel like myself anymore.
truthfully i haven't for quite some time,
but i do know,
i was different once.
i can feel myself drifting apart,
sneaking away.
diluting myself
to please their taste buds.
i'm fading.
thinning.
disappearing.
i've become rough,
ridged,
around the edges;
please don't come too close.
you don't want to see what is inside.
i'm not sure when this all began,
it all feels like a blur from
this viewpoint.
the nostalgia for my prior
days has taken over.
i can't remember what it
feels like to be wild,
or recklessly free.
i once was courageously and
unapologetically myself.
one thing i do know though is,
i was once better than this.

i am still longing
for you.
i am homesick
for your touch.

- lost

but none of these
paths lead back
to you.

*- **dead ends***

soft.

my love is
exhausted.

my heart is
worn down.

i received the bad
end of this bargain,
while you were handed
the easy way out.
unharmed and unmarked.
restful nights,
you fall asleep the
instant your head touches
your cigarette scented pillow.
tossing and turning,
i can't get you out of my mind.
i am sleepless at the
notion of who you were,
compared to who you
turned out to be.
was i important to you?
or was i just another
one of your pastimes?
another method of
escaping those lonely nights?

when she kisses you,
does she taste me
on your lips?
admit how you like the
way i've lingered on your
breath this entire time.
my name will always live
on the tip of your tongue.
has she realized
wherever she goes,
i've visited first?
don't you remember?
it was me who initially
discovered the steaming
temptation of your body.
how could you not recall?
we do not ever forget
our first loves.
she is merely trespassing,
unwelcome in my
charted city.

you were a tornado.
and it seems i
couldn't
handle your storm.

- defeat

*i'm done longing for
the things that
will never truly
be mine.*

- acceptance

soft.

you are the
oxygen
for my lungs.

i am starving
for your breath.

everyone since you has
been a dampened down
version of who you used to be.
i see you in their pitiful eyes,
starting back at me.
they never say the
right things the way you did,
or touch me in the places
i need to be touched.
i've fallen prisoner to your love,
marking down the
days until my release.
i want my freedom back.
i'm yearning to abandon
the trap of your captivity.

soft.

those eyes.
i would submerge
in his oceans
just to feel the blue
hues of his eyes again.

please don't tell me you are fine.
i can see behind those eyes
straight through every lie.
you cannot hide your spirit from me.
i've seen more of you than most,
felt your heart beat from the inside.
come here and let me rebuild you.

i'll make all this hurt go away.

we weren't
the right people at the wrong time
or the wrong people at the right time.
you were exactly what i wanted,
and i was more than you needed.
we helped create each other,
which is more than most people
manage to do for another.
love came too easily to us.
we took each other for granted,
not realizing what we had
until it was too far away to return
back into our greedy hands.
now staring back at the
past doesn't hurt like it used to.
i guess they were right;
time fixes all.

we took
things too far.

i could point fingers,
but blood is painted
on both of our hands.

- *wounded*

you took my words
with you as you left.
i've been living in
subtitles ever since.

- ***i cannot wait to***
have my voice back

most nights,
i fall asleep in
the arms of
your memory.

and most nights,
it's enough.

oh,
sweet girl.
i see your heart,
the cracks don't look as deep from here.
you feel shattered as if everything has stopped
working.
you thought you found the one,
yet he's nowhere to be found.
you lost him.
or maybe he lost you.
either way,
he's gone,
while you're here alone.
and now you feel like you're burning alive,
covered from head to toe in flames.
you've managed to put out his fire,
but in the process,
you have turned yourself off.
you've shut down.
given up.
love don't have the same ring as it used to.
they keep telling you to keep your head up,
and to be patient.
or that it will happen when you're least
expecting it.
and i hate to say it,
but they are right.
i know,
it's the last thing you want to hear.
and no,
it won't help take this agony away.
but for what it's worth,
love is out there...

someone is waiting around,
looking,
hoping,
and praying for someone like you.
and once you find each other,
it will feel like the whole
universe stopped just for you two.
you will smile,
laugh,
and cry because turns out
they were right.

thank goodness,
they were actually right.

i wish moving on was
as easy as moving out.
packed bags,
empty drawers,
blank walls.
never looking back,
only overdue goodbyes.
but there is no
easy way to let go.
you must give it time,
give yourself time.
in the meanwhile renovate,
redecorate,
remodel.

just because the love is over,
does not mean it is the
end of everything.

i keep running
back into the arms
that broke me,
hoping for healing.

- destructive behavior

*you keep damaging me,
then turning around
and calling it love.*

- the destruction

you are tattooed head-to-toe
with all the empty promises
that left you broken.
words spoken by all the
people who said they'd never leave,
but did.
you are not damaged,
or a mess.
you are simply soft in nature,
and naive enough to think
others are as well.

soft.

i'm in need of a little extra love today.

i waited for years for
you to come back,
playing that moment
in my head on repeat.
oh the irony,
that once i didn't
need you anymore,
you showed up at
my front door.
it seems you are too late.
this life,
my world,
has no place for you.

time is a peculiar thing,
and for once,
it was on my side.

and that was the thing about her,
she kept on surviving.
with bullet holes in her lungs,
and knife marks etched into her back.
she never let anything get in her way,
resilient.
a fighter,
not by choice,
but a warrior at heart.

her silence will tell you everything.

you will never be foreign.
i've seen too much,
gone farther than most.
your fingerprints are
stamped all over my skin.
there is no denying you
once trespassed here.
your footprints left dirt tracks,
and i can't clean up your mess.
even though we will
never return to the
lovers we once knew,
our past will stay a part of us.
we could never be strangers.
i have not forgotten you,
and with that,
i hope you still think of me.

did the storm of
my love frighten you?

is that why you left?

was i really too
much to weather?

losing myself
because of you
wasn't a fair trade.

sometimes
she had the
saddest eyes.
the type of
eyes you could
drown in.

- sink

when i fall,

i drown.

*- **dense***

soft.

some mornings,
just the thought of you
makes my entire day.
other mornings,
your thought is the reason
i stay in bed all day.

today, will you give me joy
or take it all away?

she was so
beautifully lost,
searching for
herself
in all the places the
universe took her.
following signs,
looking for any
glimpse of clarity.
for someone who
was so misplaced,
she carried around
a lot more
strength than
they ever knew.

soft.

perhaps i will
spend the rest
of my life
chasing people
who remind me
of you.

*- you've forever
ruined me*

*i've given up
on finding love.*

*it will come to
me when it's
ready.*

*- **surrender***

life is hard,
i know.
it's a never-ending roller
coaster of ups and downs.
highs and lows.
and sometimes we
get motion sickness,
nauseous.
we hit our tipping point,
wanting to make it stop.
get off the ride,
take a break,
and settle our stomachs for a bit.
but it never ends.
life keeps moving.
the earth keeps turning.
and yes,
it is hard.
so damn hard.
but whatever you do,
just hold on.
please do not let go.
please do not give up.

soft.

i still look at the sea and think of you.

you'll never know
true respect
and tenderness until you
accidently stumble across it.
this is why so many
of us are struggling.
we have excepted the lesser.
the nonsense.
we have subconsciously
convinced ourselves
it's the best we will get.
granted-
it's all we have
ever known.
it's what we have
always received.

unbelievable.

trust me when i say,
you deserve more.
but you already knew that.
there is better out there.
i promise.
you just have to want
it bad enough.
go out and find what
you deserve.
you won't regret it.

oh love.

how you make
such fools out of us.

there was nothing
romantic about
our lost love.

it was a tragedy.

i'm still trying to
recover from what
is left of you.

tomorrow we
will be history.
old news.
we will be past lovers,
erased words,
fading memories.
you and i will be two
people who used to know
the constellations
of one another,
but are now terrified
of the evening sky.

so please,
hold me throughout
the night.
just one more time.

i never want
tomorrow to come.

there is no pain greater
than losing the one you love,
only to watch them move on
and find someone else.
so you sit with nothing
but your thoughts,
wondering what is wrong with you,
or why you weren't good enough?
but here's the truth;
there is nothing wrong with you.
nothing would have made them stay,
or changed their minds.
love shouldn't have to be
convinced to remain.
true love doesn't need to be lost
before its' value is determined.

she's a savage,
ruthless.
cold-hearted,
not giving a damn about
anyone but herself.
selfish,
they call her.

but for those who have
seen past the walls,
she is held prisoner behind,
they understand
she's just a sad girl,
with a thousand
fragments which used
to signify her gentle heart.

in the end-

letting go turned
into giving up.
giving up turned
into losing each other.
losing each other turned
into losing ourselves.

you look at her the same way
you once stole glances at me,
as if she's the most beautiful
thing you've laid eyes on.
you made her the star of your play,
placing her on center stage.
somehow i've suddenly
become her shadow,
an understudy,
second-string.
waiting on standby,
behind closed curtains,
patiently hoping to see if
i have made the part.

you are bullet
wounds in my bones,
scar-tissue on my heart.

you are everything lost,
and everything forever
forgotten.

soft.

i'm crazy about you,

turned into,

you drive me crazy.

i'm drenched
in alcohol.
my blood as
thin as water.
i'm treading to
keep above the
surface,
but i'm too drunk
off of agony to
swim.
i want,
need,
to get sober.
but i'm unwillingly
addicted to the
pain.

he came with
the spring,
but left with
the summer.

he was seasonal.
i crave eternity.

- the fall

this terrible
nightmare,
living without you,
never seems to end

- insomnia

we have all been
warned about
bad boys and
their danger.
but i think it's
broken boys
we should stay
away from.

because in time,
they will also
destroy you.

when they ask me
about my scars,
i will tell them about
the boy with the
stubborn heart
and sad smile.
i'll explain how he took
so much of me.
how he carved his name
in the veins on my heart.
i will tell them all about
the boy who started this all.
the boy who left,
got lost,
and never found his
way back to me.

i want to unlearn the taste of your lungs.

we take hours to reply.
show interest,
but not too much.
be available,
but play hard to get.
open ourselves up,
but not show them the real us.
be casual.
don't expect anything serious.
stick to the guidelines.
we must follow these rules
if we want to play along.

we have made love into a game,
yet no one seems to win.

true love comes around
very rarely.
many of us want it so badly,
we create the prospect in
places it doesn't exist.
cramming and shoving
ourselves into people who
do not have the room for us.
and this is when the
danger begins.
in pure desperations,
we start chipping parts of
ourselves away.
giving up essential pieces
of our beings to fit into
these contorted spaces.
we should not lose ourselves
in the name of love,
we should not bury ourselves alive
for the slightest idea of it.

watch out for the
people who will try to
extinguish your fire.

they are not worthy
of your flames.

not too many people have
taken the time to open me up,
unfold me.
they've been too scared of
getting cut on my rigid edges,
thin paper cuts.
small but deep.
a sharp,
yet dull pain.
they have made me feel
as if i'm not legible;
a book not worth reading,
a novel gone unnoticed.

we can break overnight,
but healing takes eternity.
and the truth is,
there are some things
we cannot mend from,
or completely recover from.
things we cannot overcome.

perhaps some pains aren't
meant to be left behind.

i can see her abandoned love
in those grey eyes.
he took too much life from her.
he never deserved her soft heart.
her wild soul.
she was strong,
and he simply could
not handle her aftermath.

i want you to
fall for my soul,
not my body.
to see me for
what i've hidden
on the inside,
not what i've painted
on the outside.
i want you to know
me for who i am,
not who you
want me to be.

perception
is such a
dangerous thing.

i will be your
everything
or your
nothing.

i am not
one for
undefined
in-betweens.

- millennial love

*perhaps if i keep
telling myself i
don't need love,
maybe one day
i'll wake and it
will be the truth.*

*- i don't need it.
i don't need it.
i don't need it.*

they should not ask
you to change for them.
they will not make you
feel little or small,
unwanted,
not good enough.
they should be accepting
and supportive.
they should think you are
perfect just the way you are.

because you are.

what a cruel joke
the universe can play;
giving you everything
you've ever wanted,
only to then tear it away.

it's hard to put
yourself out there.
vulnerability looks so
beautiful on us all,
but we've convinced
ourselves differently.
so we hide behind
our emotions,
swallowing the truth to
help hinder the pain.
hoping it will lessen
the contact of the fall.
since when did it
become the norm to
hurt the ones we love?

this whole breaking
thing never seems
to get easier.

this whole loving
thing never seems
to end well.

you were the one my heart
wanted to call her own.
you were the one my heart
couldn't bear to lose.
you were the one she wanted
to believe in.
she needed to believe in.

you were the lesson my heart
was too stubborn to learn.

you are a subtle
ache in my spine.
the type of pain
that fades with
the season,
but never truly
goes away.

you are gone,
yet somehow
always here.

you have brought me so much pain,
there is no denying it.
perfectly wrapping
your spell around my neck,
suffocating me with every trick.
but with time,
i have healed.
i've finished grieving,
rejoicing the relief of your departure.
i don't think of you as often as i used to.
i don't crave your touch,
or long for your tainted memories.
your heart has evaded mine.
completely.
no part of you
lingers inside of me,
you are not welcome
here anymore.
i've moved on,
leaving all your pieces behind.
one day,
i will meet a man who will replace you.
he will give me the love i so
undyingly craved from you,
filling the voids left within,
fitting perfectly in the
spaces left behind.
on that day,
you will feel the pain i once felt.
he will be everything you are not.
and you will be nothing to me.

you've made me into
the woman i stand as today,
not in the way i fell to
my knees for you,
but the manner i stood
on my own two feet as you
used yours to walk away.
i fixed myself,
not needing you to stay
around for long.
i understand now how
all i needed was
your departure.
i needed you to walk away
in order for me to
learn how to love freely.
so please darling,
stop apologizing for leaving.
it was one of the best things
to happen to me.

soft.

i crave a love that sinks oceans.

bruised knees,
weak grasp;
i'm still
praying for
you and i.

soft.

and all i want,
is to fall asleep
in your arms.
one.
last.
time.

kiana azizian

the
softening.

kiana azizian

you left. gone.
and i've spent too much time missing you.
trying to wrap my mind around this mess,
and all these unanswered
questions living in my head.
i let your chaos wreck my peace of mind.
thinking you were the one for me,
i convinced myself it was true love.
but i couldn't quite understand
why you didn't see it too.
now the pieces that used to fit
seem to be from different puzzles.
we are on different pages, in different books.
i see why we didn't work.
you've settled down,
and i've never been one to settle.
i fight for the things i want,
while you've proven to
give up when things become difficult.
in a way,
we've skipped the messy bits.
and in ten years' time,
i won't wake up next to you,
resenting our life together,
and you won't taste the
guilt of holding me back.
this was for the better.
thank you for all you've taught me
about love and loss.
heartbreak and redemption.
i thought you'd be the end of me.
but turns out,
you were just the fundamental
beginning of my astounding debut.

the key to a
happy life is
to stay soft
in this dense
world.

the truth is,
we will all get our hearts
broken at some point
during our lifetime.
we will break,
fall apart,
and even shatter.
we will wake up in the morning
with a pair of matching black eyes
and lips dripping of somber,
asking ourselves,
who have i become,
or
how did i get here?
but in the end,
all that truly matters is
the way we repair
our broken souls.
how we mend,
rise above,
and come back together.

i'm still
learning
slowly
how to
let you
go.

- *progress*

i'm still
slowly
learning
how to
fight for
myself.

- ***progress II***

she was braver
than most knew,
always doubting,
belittling herself for
the sake of others.
she has spent too much
time chasing toxic people,
looking for harmony
within the midst of chaos.
they've unfairly convinced
her she wasn't good enough.
i guess this was the
price she paid for carrying
a big heart in a little world.

wild things
are not meant
to be tamed.

it wasn't until he walked
away when i realized
i needed to stop placing
my happiness in the
arms of others.
people leave,
and they often disappoint.
so i reached inside,
and pulled out everything
i'd always been expecting
to receive from the others.

i must find contentment
on my own.

it is the only way.

and what would you do if you
knew anything was possible?

what are the things that keep
you up at night?

tell me what makes your bones shatter,
and what makes them cave?

the day you completely
evaded my being,
i smiled at my heart,
and whispered-

we did it.

we didn't end up together,
but i am still glad we met.
you cut me open,
tore my insides from
top to bottom.
you shattered my core and
taught me how to bleed.
you killed me,
allowing me to
bring myself back to life.

soft.

live wildly.
fall willingly.
love softly.

when your
heart
is heavy,
forgive.
release all
the unnecessary
weight.

- necessity

*there is beauty
in letting go.*

*there is strength
in moving on.*

***- find you beauty.
find your strength***

soft.

in time,
you will mend.
for now,
lie next to me.
take down
your walls.

let's start
with an easy one,

*tell me all
the things
you wished
you'd said?*

i'm still healing,
yet not quite there.
there are many
things i'm not sure of,
but one thing i know,
you will not be the end of me.

there is an unsettledness in
always being too much.
people can rarely handle you.
they make you feel like you're
not worth their time or energy.
there comes a point
when you will consider
turning yourself off,
solely for the sake of others.
i ask you one thing,
please keep yourself on.
if anything,
turn yourself up.
louder.
life was not meant
to be lived on mute.
blast yourself,
and forget anyone who
tries to change your settings.
it's not your fault little
people cannot handle big things.

let her light carry you home.

she is destined
for the stars.
not even the moon
can stand in her way.

we are only as broken
as we convince ourselves.
brokenness is a state of mind.

and so is healing.

in the end,
you will only regret the
love you didn't give.
locking up your heart,
keeping it safe,
isn't really protecting it.
truthfully,
you are only hurting yourself.
fall madly,
and trust someone will
be standing at the bottom,
ready to catch all of your soul.

you must
tell your story.

the universe
deserves
to hear
your magic.

she was so
envious
of the sea,
how it roared
so wildly.
so free.

- untamed

she
is
proof
peace
can come
from madness.

- serenity

i hated myself so much,
i chased anything that
would get me the slightest
bit of attention,
often finding myself in
the wrong arms,
the wrong beds,
wondering why i was
never good enough for these men.
years passed by living this way,
until i finally woke up in
my own company,
and realized this was
all i really needed.

the softness you
carry around with
you is stunning.

please never
take it off.

we're all struggling,
fighting our own
battles within,
and doing what we
need to survive.

be kind to one another;
it is the only thing we can
do to help ease the pain
of this unkind world.

soft.

there's a beauty
in being lost.
there's a beauty
in being unfound.

we fall.
we break.
we fail.

but then,

we rise.
we heal.
we overcome.

even when you're
not at your best,
the right person will
stand with you.
they will accept
your flaws and
appreciate their
beauty by painting
them on the walls.
the right person will not
give up when things get hard.
they will fight even harder.
they will put in the work,
the effort.
they will never make you feel
as if you are not good enough.

and if they do
not do these things,
well then maybe they're
not the person you
thought they are.

the sun never
forgets me.
even when
i have lost
myself.

this,
is the beginning
of loving yourself.

welcome home.

unravel.

into something greater
than before.

unravel.

into something stronger
than you've ever been.

soft.

when they stop
bringing you
happiness-
that is when
you should
walk away.

love runs
through
my veins.

i am made of it.

your kind touch,
and gentle soul;
it's what got
you here.
be thankful for
carrying the world
in your heart.

i will make these
words dance
until they find
their way back
to you.

the truth is:

some people are not
meant to be forgotten.

some pains are
not meant to heal.

some loves are
not meant to be lost.

take the weight of
the world off your
wings darling.
and fly far,
far away from here.

we're always told
there's a romanticism in
holding on to toxic love,
and never letting it go.
even when it is tearing us
apart from the cells of our jaw.
so we cling and grasp onto
these relationships until we're
hanging on to nothing
but a dwindling thread.
they've convinced us
fighting makes us strong,
and it will all be worth
it in the end.
but this is the furthest
from the truth.
love does not involve killing
ourselves for the
sake of another,
it is waking up each
morning with your hopes
and dreams lying right
next to you.

looking for
validation
in others
is the best
way to feel
unworthy.

soft.

i don't know how
the sun does it.
losing herself to the
darkness every night;
only to rise,
shine,
and light up the
morning sky.

allow
yourself
to fall apart.

then allow
yourself
to come back
together.

- restoration

*good things
leave.*

*yet good things
often stay.*

*- **equilibrium***

soft.

you have too
much thunder
inside of you
to be anything
but extraordinary.

kiana azizian

what do you think love is like?

*like slow dancing,
under the stars,
to no music.*

she is falling.
she is learning.
understanding.

she is doing
the best she can.

we don't give up
on the ones we love.

we fight like hell
until there's nothing
left to give.

this is how we should
love one another.

soft.

i just need
someone who
knows how to
hold me back
together when
i fall apart.

love yourself
so fully that the
pain won't have
any place to live.

soft.

it's in the eyes.

always the eyes.

you will never
destroy the
soft in me.

- resilient

*i no longer
cave at the
whisper of
your name.*

- recovery

oh, the way
these poems
speak to you.

they were
written just
for you.

i will not thank
you for this
strength.
this force,
this power,
it was all me.

soft.

you are a
revolution.

the entire
universe has
been waiting
for you.

running from your
heart will do
you no good.
for one day,
you will wake up to
realize you have
lost everything.
and you will be left
with nothing.
stay around for
the people who
spark your fire.

fight for the love you
know you deserve.

they will not
define you.

they never can,
and never will.

i hope you do not
give them that
type of power.

she wore her
scars as trophies.

tragedy never
looked so beautiful.

even the
strongest
of us breaks
from time
to time.

we're just
human
at the end
of the day.

sometimes people
don't come back.

and sometimes
that's okay.

the day you left,
i did not feel grief.

i felt relief.

- *release*

i'm
unraveling
you
from
my
skin.

- freedom

this breaking.
this healing.
this loving.
this leaving.

my goodness,
it's all a bit messy.

soft.

i'm finished
fighting for
someone who
is already gone.

take your shoes off.
let your hair down.
relax.
unwind.
you've been strong
for too long my dear.

from time to time,
it's okay to let your
heart out to play.

it's safe here.

after
everything i've
put her through,
my heart still
whispers,
begs:

please do not give up on love.

soft.

i am most true
to myself with
a broken heart
and a heavy soul.

- *vulnerability*

*a heart that has
been broken is
one that has
known true love.*

- **privilege**

there are different
types of love.

some loves will rip
you to shreds,
making you question
your essences.

the other type of love
will come so easily;
it will make you
question how love
could be anything else.

you cannot
grow out
from the
weeds of
bitterness.

be soft,
even when
it seems
impossible.

once the confusion settles,
the calm will come.

you must be patient.

soft.

stop looking
for love.

let it come
find you.

allow yourself
to feel the oceans
that rage inside
of you.

stop being so careful with your heart.
it is okay to let it out of its cage,
to roam free.
send it out into the universe.
see what happens,
or who it finds.
hearts were meant for breaking.
and with that,
they were made for healing.
we must see how far love will take us,
even if we get damaged along the way.
a scarred heart is stronger
than a safe one;
more cherished.
a heart must find itself in
the wrong hands once or twice,
before it finds a home in the right palms.

i am done feeling
inadequate due to
the lack of a man
in my life.

love me or lose me.

i'm not settling for
anything in between.

we'll do anything
to be saved;
to let someone,
anyone in.
so we drink their poison,
knowing they are the thing
that is killing us,
yet liking the way their
pain burns in the spaces
left unattended.

this type of love will
scar you forever.

but at least,
this way,
we will always
remember.

when you cannot
be brave or strong,
be love.
it will lead you back
home to yourself.

come close.

show me your scars.
let us heal together.

you will never be alone.
because you have the sea,
and you always have me.

soft.

your past
has no grasp
over you.

- let it flee

open up,
and look
inside.

restore.
mend.
rejoice.

- how to rebuild

people like you
are not easily
forgotten.

people like you
last a lifetime.

soft.

if you
remain
silent for
too long,
you will
forget the
sound of
your own
voice.

- scream

*love is the
answer to
every question
your heart
screams.*

- listen closely

you must open
your heart,
so love can
know where to
find you.

sometimes,
your heart will
be too heavy for
others to carry.

this my love,
is why you must
learn to bear it on
your own.

find your wild.

hold it tight.

never let it go.

i found solitude in myself,
understanding the
importance of putting
my own needs before others.
it all makes sense now,
i was looking for me in
all the wrong places.
i was searching for adoration
in all the wrong people.

that heavy heart
and those sad eyes;
they are what make
you beautiful.
they are what make
you even more
human than the
rest of us.

the sun
surrenders
to the dark
every night.

this is the
type of
devotion
i need.

you were kind
and gentle
before they
came around
and convinced you
you weren't enough.

don't you remember?

i've come to learn
the difficult way,
just because we
desire someone,
doesn't mean
we're supposed to
end up with them.

i hope
you've found
contentment.

i'm still
searching
for mine.

soft.

i've lived too fast
fallen too far,
given too much.

yet i've ended up
exactly where i
want to be.

the moment you
find yourself,
i hope all you
feel is peace.

the one who
broke you,
will never be
the one
to heal you.

- they cannot do both

we're searching
for restoration in
broken people.

**- two wrongs never
made a right**

your soft is important.

never forget this.

and as the birds
danced with
the flowers,
the sun smiled
down at them.
love was in the air.
she could just feel it.

moving on is
a brave thing.

find the courage
to let go,
and finally allow
yourself to fly freely.

soft.

perhaps,
i'll meet you on the other side of all this.

tonight,
the stars have
my lips,
and the moon
has my heart.

we must take what
we can from this earth.
the kind word from a stranger,
a message from a long-lost friend,
hot cups of coffee,
waking up before your morning alarm,
sunshine on a winter day,
someone remembering your favorite color,
unexpected flowers,
spontaneous kisses,
coming home after a long trip away,
childhood friends,
printed photographs,
a hand-written letter in the mail,
driving with no set destination,
spending all day in bed watching old movies,
cookies & cream ice cream,
finding someone who makes
your heart beat a little faster,
a good book you cannot put down.

at the end of the day,
these are the only
things that matter.
they are what get us
through the day,
and help get us
through this life.

oh,
the little things.

break open.
let the negativity flow out.
pour out.
grieve.
pull yourself
back together,
and breathe.

listen here:
you are not
broken,
inadequate,
or helpless.

you are
whole,
important,
and healing.

- affirmation

we may not
be perfect.

but we are so,
so enough.

- reassurance

i have cut myself
off from everything
holding me down.
i feel more myself
than ever before.
finally,
i can breathe.

i am free.

*s*ometimes
*o*pening up to the
*f*eelings is
*t*ough.

i am s.o.f.t. again.